D1447618

Gallery Books
Editor: Peter Fallon

OAR

Moya Cannon

OAR

Gallery Books

This revised edition of
Oar
is first published
in paperback
on 11 May 2000.

The Gallery Press
Loughcrew
Oldcastle
County Meath
Ireland

*All rights reserved. For permission
to reprint or broadcast these poems
write to The Gallery Press.*

© Moya Cannon 1990, 2000

ISBN 1 85235 263 9 (*paperback*)

The Gallery Press acknowledges the financial assistance
of An Chomhairle Ealaíon / The Arts Council, Ireland,
and the Arts Council of Northern Ireland.

Contents

for my parents

You must take a well-cut oar and go on till you reach a people who know nothing of the sea and never use salt with their food, so that our crimson-painted ships and the long oars that serve those ships as wings are quite beyond their ken.
— *The Odyssey*, trans. E. V. Rieu

PART ONE

Eagles' Rock

Predators and carrion crows still nest here,
falcons, and this pair of ravens
that I first heard when I reached the cairn
and noticed a narrow skull among the stones.

Here, further east at the cliff,
their wing-tips touch the rock below me,
and leave,
and touch again.

Black as silk, they know their strong corner of the sky.
They circle once
and once
and once
and once again and soar out
to sweep their territory of bright grey hills.

There are green slashes down there,
full of wells and cattle,
and higher places, where limestone, fertile,
catacombed, breaks into streams and gentians.

Predators have nested here in late winter,
have swung against this face —
feather arrogant against stone —
long enough to name it.

Once Colman, the dove saint,
lived under this cliff,
left us his oratory, his well,
and his servant's grave.

The eagles are hunted, dead,
but down among the scrub and under the hazels
this summer's prey tumbles already
out of perfect eggs.

Blossom Viewing in the Burren

From below
we mistook them for cattle.
When we reach the cliff's edge
the long-backed beasts
are thorn trees,
bent above a limestone wall.

Under the wall
young bushes clump together in the sun.
Today there is no breeze
and, where trees have outgrown their shelter,
limbs, dragged east by prevailing winds,
are white and drunk with summer.

To the top of the wall
the oldest tree grows, as thick as a man's neck,
then it withers to the east,
a black stick,
a seed's fragile gallows.

Life here is unredeemed
unless, in bitter winter,
a tree can know again in its still sap
these weeks of blossoming,
this perfect unfolding.

Soon again, the flower will fall before the red seed
and the red seed will fall without judgement;
nothing will be judged,
    the skinning wind,
    the wall built to keep beasts safe,
    or the generous, deceiving earth.

Holy Well

Water returns, hard and bright,
out of the faulted hills.

Rain that flowed
down through the limestone's pores
until dark streams hit bedrock
now finds a way back,
past the roots of the ash,
to a hillside pen
of stones and statues.

Images of old fertilities
testify to nothing more, perhaps,
than the necessary miracle
of water trapped and stored
in a valley where water is fugitive.

A chipped and tilted Mary
grows green among rags and sticks.
Her trade dwindles —
bad chests, rheumatic pains,
the supplications, mostly, and the confidences of old age.

Yet sometimes,
swimming out in waters
that were blessed in the hill's labyrinthine heart,
the eel flashes past.

Diarmuid and Grainne's Beds

These dolmens
were death's doors, death's tables.
They were wrested from the earth
to shelter hoards of bones.

But memory faltered,
or mind capered,
and a story spread
that these were the beds
of lovers.

Handwritten annotations:

slowly turned used some kind of st—

tomb 🐚

shape of it

store of valuables secretly hidden

usually

in a lively or playful way

forcibly pulled

stones that were to struggle to pull from ground

(ablir)

skip/dance about

gambader : sat envolée

Paulnabrone is a portal tomb in the Burren that is a popular tourist attraction.

Irish folktale so important to culture it became apart of elementary curriculum in Ireland.

Thirst in the Burren

No ground or floor
is as kind to the human step
as the rain-cut flags
of these white hills.

Porous as skin,
limestone resounds sea-deep, time-deep,
yet, in places, rainwater has worn it thin
as a fish's fin.

From funnels and clefts
ferns arch their soft heads. → human characteristics to nature

A headland full of water, dry as bone,
with only thirst as a diviner,
thirst of the inscrutable fern
and the human thirst
that beats upon a stone.

West

Between high walls
the grass grows greenest.
These limestone walls have no need of gates.
The room-sized fields,
with their well made gaps,
open onto one another
in a great puzzle
of fragile wall and pasture
and more gaps.

Only occasionally will we find
an animal caught
in a cropped field
without gate or gap.

Maritime Relationship

Oar

Walk inland and inland
with your oar,
until someone asks you
what it is.

Then build your house.

new perspective on home

For only then will you need to tell and (know)
that the sea is immense and unfathomable,
that the oar that pulls
against the wave
and with the wave
is (everything.)

only way to survive

puts value in home

Thalassa

Having got up, decided to go home,
how often do we find ourselves
walking in the wrong direction.

Some echo under the stones
seduces our feet,
leads them down again
by the grey, agitated sea.

'Taom'

[handwritten: — Irish language opening the following landscape]

[handwritten: to tide]

The unexpected tide,
the great wave,
uncontained, breasts the rock,
overwhelms the heart, in spring or winter.

Surfacing from a fading language,
the word comes when needed.
A dark sound surges and ebbs,
its accuracy steadying the heart.

Certain kernels of sound
reverberate like seasoned timber,
unmuted truths of a people's winters,
stirrings of a thousand different springs.

There are small unassailable words *[handwritten: inattackable]*
that diminish Caesars;
territories of the voice
that intimate across death and generation
how a secret was imparted —
that first articulation,
when a vowel was caught
between a strong and a tender consonant,
when someone, in anguish
made a new and mortal sound
that lived until now,
a testimony
to waves succumbed to
and survived.

Tree Stump

Thrown up
on the stones
in a bad November,

tree stump
returned from an exile
amongst fish and cormorants.

For a week or a year
the ocean has salted your huge wound,
rocks have battered off your bark,
but the shipworms haven't riddled you.

Alive or dead,
there is little left of the slow strength
that filled a sky
when summer followed winter
and wind threw down the seeds.

I drag off bladderwrack
to look at the years
and find, hugged hard in the wilderness of your roots,
lumps of granite
that stunted
and informed your growth.

Turf Boats

Black hookers at anchor
shining sea cattle;
rough trees for masts
rooted in salt water;
built, not for slaughter,
but for a life-giving traffic.

Wide ribs of oak,
a human heart filled you
as you sailed out of Carna.
You came into Kilronan,
two sods went flying,
you carried fire to the islands,
lime to Connemara.

Hollow boats at the Claddagh,
hearts that beat in you
lie in granite-walled graveyards
from Leitirmullen to Barna,
finished with hardship,
the unloading of cargo,
the moody Atlantic —
that entered the marrow,
and bright days off Ceann Boirne,
when wind struck the brown sails
and Ithaca was Carna.

PART TWO

Prodigal

Dark mutter tongue,
rescue me,
I am drawn into outrageous worlds
where there is no pain or innocence,
only the little quiet sorrows
and the elegant joys of power.

Someone
businesslike in his desires
has torn out the moon by its roots.
Oh, my tin king is down now, mother,
down and broken,
my clear-browed king
who seemed to know no hungers
has killed himself.
Old gutter mother,
I am bereft now,
my heart has learnt nothing
but the stab of its own hungers
and the murky truth of a half-obsolete language
that holds at least the resonance
of the throbbing, wandering earth.

Try to find me stones and mud now, mother,
give me somewhere to start,
green and struggling, a blade under snow,
for this place and age demand relentlessly
something I will never learn to give.

No Sense in Talking

What knot at the root of articulation is loosening,
have we said too much?
The old trees are coming down to the river to drink
and the young trees on the mountain
are tormented by this, their first autumn.
Who now can plant a finger on the loss
or deny the bereavement?

We thought only to bring clarity
out of the murk of utterance,
a modicum of control,
a necessary precision
and, perhaps, an elegance.

But we find
that in this damned garden by the river
we have bred pheasants;
it hardly matters whether we feed them or shoot.

Where now is the fine drive of abstraction,
where our dim talk on pillows?
Where are our black ships at anchor?
And, above all, of what use is it to us to know
that the old dirty languages still hold
touch in the ear,
lick in the ear,
secrets for everybody?

We are no longer everybody.
Half-individuated we suffer,
unable to assuage the hungers
in the head, the heart, the blood.
Our dreams differ now,
one from the other,

so that we cannot converse on pillows
and our gods quarrel endlessly.

We, who have conquered,
weep dry tears,
unable to lament our loss —
the tongue's tangle
of comfort and fear.

We know well that
if we had sense we would know
that the river is stealing the bank,
tugging it down streams by the long grass,
while under our feet,
leaves lie that are red as dragons
and the very stones are ambiguous.

Have we said too little
too clearly,
our parsimony a theft?
Who now is there to assert
that there was love among the barbarous daffodils
when leaves were green as spears?

Hills

My wild hills come stalking.
Did I perhaps after all, in spite of all,
try to cast them off,
my dark blue hills,
that were half the world's perimeter?
Have I stooped so low as to lyricise about heather,
adjusting my love
to fit elegantly
within the terms of disinterested discourse?

Who do I think I'm fooling?
I know these hills better than that.
I know them blue, like delicate shoulders.
I know the red grass that grows in high boglands
and the passionate brightnesses and darknesses
of high bog lakes.
And I know too how,
in the murk of winter,
these wet hills will come howling through my blood
like wolves.

Ultramontane

The questions lay in the soft green book
each with its answer.
Who made the world?

We learnt to love a garden
with trees full of soft fruit
while, outside, the wind ripped at briars.

And when spring came
we cut rushes
to weave crosses.

The Foot of Muckish

People from our town on the coast
cut turf at the foot of Muckish.
Other than that,
it was beyond our pale.

But one evening, coming down off Muckish
when I was ten, a clumsy, dark-hearted child,
I came over the last shoulder
and the small black mountain opposite
rose up in a cliff
and rocked a lake between its ankles.

A sixpence,
a home for all the little dark streams,
a moon
in the miles of acid land.

Listening Clay

for Caitriona

There are sounds
that we can,
and do, trust;

    a gale in the trees,
    the soft click of stones, where the tide falls back,
    a baby crying in the night.

No one has ever mocked these sounds,
or tried to comprehend them.
They are too common to be bought or sold,
they were here before the word,
and have no significance in law.

Endlessly repeated,
immutable,
they are sounds without a history.
They comfort and disturb
the clay part of the heart.

Easter

We went down through gardens where the trees moved,
the gates to the swamp were thrown open
and we were lost to the sprouting earth.

We were down among the old easters
where passion unmade us into our elements.
In that warm dark, only the blind heart ploughed on
as though the terrain were known.

Scar

Why does it affect
and comfort me,
the little scar,
where, years ago, you cut your lip
shaving when half-drunk
and in a hurry
to play drums in public.

We step now
to rhythms we don't own or understand
and, with blind, dog-like diligence,
we hunt for scars
in tender places.

Eros

To be with you, my love,
is not at all like being in heaven
but like being in the earth.

Like hazelnuts
we sleep
and dream faint memories of a life
when we were high, green, among leaves;
a life given
in a time of callow innocence,
before storms came
and we all fell down,
rattled down cold streams,
caught in the stones,
while berries, seasons, flowed past.
Then quicker currents, elvers, dislodged us,
nudged us out into the flow,
rushed us down with black leaf-debris,
and swept on
forgetting us
on some river-bend or delta.

For us, drifted together,
this is the time when shells are ready
for that gentler breaking.

The deep and tender earth
assails us with dreams,
breaks us,
nourishes us,
as we tug apart
its own black crust.

Afterlove

for Colman

How could I have forgotten
the sickness,
the inescapability?
My strange love,
it frightens my life.
We sail high seas
and watch the voyages of stars.
Sometimes they collide.
Did you know, you make my head flame.
Blue flames and purple flames leap about my head.
I had once a thousand tongues
but tonight
my head is crashing through the sky,
my head is flaming on a dish.

My love,
carry it in carefully,
my love,
carry it in with trumpets.

PART THREE

Narrow Gatherings

At Portrush
the boarding houses are empty
even along the sea-front.
How quiet a Sunday
for after Easter.
Up to the tall houses
the pale tide flows
disturbed and beautiful,
the April sun barely brightens
its legendary cold.

Lir's children had it hardest here,
and here
the giants sculpted rock to honeycomb,
hammered back the great arched cliffs,
but failed to join two shores.

Encumbered by legend,
we are foreigners here
and know less
than we had imagined.

A band, practising in the town, winds
now out of wind-scraped streets,
the policeman first
and the great drums
that come and come like summer thunder

and then the flutes and fifes —
a music unexpected
as silver water collected
in the dark shoulders of hills, caught,
and gathered narrow for an instant
under high wrists,

until the wind splits it finely,
a young river scattering.
Under a low sun
the band is marching now
past the painted doors
and down along the promenade,
towards the cold shore and turning
until all the wind-snatched silver life strikes
bright against the tide:

And after
come the marching children,
growing smaller and smaller
in their uniforms.

Dark Spring

i.m. Feilimí Ó hUallacháin

Last night
the sky was still so full of light
the birds shouted in the empty trees
when, in the bone the dark cracked,
with so little sound,
almost no sound,
we did not hear it
but, incredulous, saw in our grief
the dark birds falling out of every tree
and after the birds the falling dead dark leaves.
Oh, we wept, we were not told,
we were not led to expect,
back when the thin bone knit to close the sky,
inside the skull-cave when we etched our myths
and later made our compacts with the ogre
we had no thought of this,
nor could we have schooled our hearts for this absurd
and sudden
sorrow.

Fair head
so vivid, in the loose wet earth.

In your death we are twice lost, twice bereaved,
all our compacts now dissolved,
we are so unexpectedly mortal.

Yet even
as we leave you
the sun flies down
to strike the dark hills green.
Defiant, it drives the pulse of summer
through this most desolate spring.

Annals

Rocks were fitted
to round the tops of narrow windows.
When they got to the doorway
the monks had chisels, *cisailler*
so they carved the faces of saints.
tailler

Moling and Fiachra,
blurred by twelve centuries,
gaze from their Romanesque arch
into the hazels,
remembering the time the mad king
came down out of the trees at last,
ate humble pie
and, with some misgivings,
took to a foreign religion.

Clapped to the church's other end,
a handball alley complete
with decayed timber seats
shares a fifteenth-century window.
The hibernian colosseum
stands derelict within the century,
hardly a cypher now in the annals
of the Kilkenny county board.

But now that the tree king, *fourmère*
and the monks, and the handball-players are dust,
the last lay recited,
the last malediction lifted,
the last protest contested,

a thrush nesting in the doorway
shifts slightly on her eggs,
and awaits the millennium.

Wet Doves

Two wet doves are perched in the tree all afternoon.

On a day as rainy as this,
a bare apple tree is a poor place to roost.

Beyond my window
this tatty metaphor of love and fructitude huddles
and grubs under its oxters
and defecates and drips
and then
spreads two perfectly white fans
and flies away.

Nest

A brown wheel of reeds and broken willow
turns somnolently in a corner above the weir.
How long will that current hold it
before the flow sweeps it over?

Two coke cans and a fast-food carton
are wound into the heart of it.

Out of habit,
god goes on making nests.

Crow's Nest

On St Stephen's day,
near the cliffs on Horn Head,
I came upon a house,
the roof-beams long since rotted into grass
and, outside, a little higher than the lintels,
a crow's nest in a dwarf tree.

A step up from the bog
into the crown of the ash,
the nest is a great tangled heart;
heather sinew, long blades of grass, wool and a feather,
wound and wrought
with all the energy and art
that's in a crow.

Did crows ever build so low before?
Were they deranged, the pair who nested here,
or the other pair who built the house behind the tree,
or is there no place too poor or wild
to support,
if not life,
then love, which is the hope of it,
for who knows whether the young birds lived?

After the Burial

They straightened the blankets,
piled her clothes onto the bed,
soaked them with petrol,
then emptied the gallon can
over the video and tape recorder,
stepped outside their trailer,
lit it, watched until only the burnt chassis was left,
gathered themselves
and pulled out of Galway.

Camped for a week in Shepherd's Bush,
then behind a glass building in Brixton,
he went into drunken mourning for his dead wife,
while their children hung around the vans,
or foraged in the long North London streets
among other children, some of whom also perhaps
    understood,
that beyond respectability's pale,
where reason and civility show their second face,
it's hard to lay ghosts.

Sympathetic Vibration

for Kathleen

'You never strike a note,
you always *take* the note.'

Did it take her many
of her eighty quiet passionate years
to earn that knowledge,
or was it given?

Music, the dark tender secret of it,
is locked into the wood of every tree.
Yearly it betrays its presence
in minute fistfuls of uncrumpling green.

No stroke or blade can release the music
which is salve to ease the world's wounds,
which tells and, modulating, retells
the story of our own groping roots,
of the deep sky from which they retreat
and, in retreating, reach —
the tree's great symphony of leaf.

No stroke or blade can bring us that release
but sometimes, where wildness has not been stilled,
hands, informed by years of patient love,
can come to know the hidden rhythms of the wood,
can touch bow to gut
and take the note,
as the heart yields and yields
and sings.

Foundations

Digging foundations for a kitchen,
a foot and a half below the old concrete
they open a midden of seashells.

This was once called 'kitchen' —
poor man's meat, salty, secretive,
gathered at low spring tide.

Blue mussels creaked as a hand twisted them from the
    cluster,
limpets were banged off with a stone, lifted with a blade,
the clam's breathing deep in wet sand
gave a mark to the spade.

Backs ached, reaping the cold and succulent harvest.
How many were consumed?

A shovelful, two shovelfuls,
six barrowloads, are dug out and dumped —
the midden runs under the wall
into the neighbour's yard.
The builder goes home, joking that he's found gold.

In a battered barrow, under the June evening sun,
the last shovelfuls turn palest gold.
They speak in silent sympathy
with all that has been exiled, killed and hidden,
then exhumed,
vulnerable again in the air of another age.

The taciturn clams break their silence to say,
'Dig us out if you need to,
position the steel,
raise the concrete walls,
but, when your shell is complete,

remember that your life,
no less than ours,
is measured by the tides of the sea
and is unspeakably fragile.'

Votive Lamp

The Pope and the Sacred Heart
went off on the back of a cart,
and I've tried to find a home
for the Child of Prague.

If that lamp weren't the exact
shape of a brandy glass there might be some chance
that I'd part with it.

Small chance, though.
If I'd been brought up in the clear light
of reason,
I might feel differently.

But I often come home in the dark
and, from the hall door,
in the red glow
I can discern
a child's violin
and, coming closer,
a plover;
the photograph of a dead friend;
three hazelnuts gathered from a well;
and three leather-skinned shamans
who flew all the way from Asia
on one card.

I designed none of this and don't know whether
sacred objects and images tend to cluster
around a constant light,
or whether
the small star's constancy,
through other lives and other nights,
now confers some sanctity
on my life's bric-à-brac.